Virtual Collaboration

20 MINUTE MANAGER SERIES

Get up to speed fast on essential business skills. Whether you're looking for a crash course or a brief refresher, you'll find just what you need in HBR's 20-Minute Manager series—foundational reading for ambitious professionals and aspiring executives. Each book is a concise, practical primer, so you'll have time to brush up on a variety of key management topics.

Advice you can quickly read and apply, from the most trusted source in business.

Titles include:

Creating Business Plans

Delegating Work

Difficult Conversations

Finance Basics

Getting Work Done

Giving Effective Feedback

Innovative Teams

Leading Virtual Teams

Other books in this series (continued):

20 MINUTE MANAGER SERIES

Virtual Collaboration

Work from anywhere
Overcommunicate
Avoid isolation

HARVARD BUSINESS REVIEW PRESS

Boston, Massachusetts

Copyright 2016 Harvard Business School Publishing Corporation

The web addresses referenced in this book were live and correct at the time of the book's publication but may be subject to change.

Library of Congress Cataloging-in-Publication Data.

Names: Harvard Business Review Press, issuing body.
Title: Virtual collaboration : work from anywhere, overcommunicate, avoid isolation.
Other titles: 20 minute manager series.
Description: Boston, Massachusetts : Harvard Business Review Press, [2016] | Series: 20 minute manager series | Include index.
Identifiers: LCCN 2016012717 (print) | LCCN 2016016129 (ebook) | ISBN 9781633691476 (pbk. : alk. paper) | ISBN 9781633691483 ()
Subjects: LCSH: Virtual work teams. | Business communication. | Telecommuting.
Classification: LCC HD66. V556 2016 (print) LCC HD66 (ebook) | DDC 658.4/022202854678—dc23
LC record available at http://lccn.loc.gov/2016012717

ISBN: 9781633691476
eISBN: 9781633691483

Preview

More of us are working more often in a location that's different from our colleagues and business partners. Maybe you log in from your home office daily or work every now and then in the quiet car of a train, or some combination of sites. Regardless of where you park your laptop, you need to work well with others to meet your professional and organizational goals. But how do you build relationships through a computer screen? What if your boss suspects that "remote work" really means no work? What do you do when your computer dies in the middle of a sensitive-feedback video chat? How do you cope with the isolation that can build when you're working on your own? This book will help you build productive relationships with colleagues while you foster your own sense of initiative—no matter where you are.

Virtual Collaboration walks you through these important basics:

- Working productively from any location

- Picking the right tools for wherever you're working, at home or on the road

- Clarifying the roles, tasks, and processes that will govern your collaboration

- Communicating effectively over a variety of media

- Getting and keeping your colleagues' attention when you're not in the same place

- Setting—and sticking to—a schedule that works for both you and your dispersed collaborators

- Keeping isolation at bay by connecting with your coworkers

- Staying motivated when the only one to administer an in-person pep talk is you

- Navigating common challenges, such as technology glitches and conflicts, over the ether

Contents

Contents

Virtual Collaboration

What Is Virtual Collaboration?

What Is Virtual Collaboration?

Few of us work every day, all day, in a traditional office anymore. We log in from clients' offices. We participate in conference calls on our commutes. We work more and more frequently with people perched at faraway desks, whom we've never met.

Virtual collaboration is the new norm. For the purpose of this book, *virtual collaboration* means all the work we do with others when we don't see them face to face. You're a virtual collaborator if you:

- Work outside an office regularly, full or part time

- Work from home in a pinch, because of bad weather or to wait for a contractor, care for a sick child, change your scenery, or get more done

- Travel regularly, but need to stay in touch with your team back home

- Are on a short-term assignment away from your usual workplace

The "virtual" part of these arrangements arises in how you interact with the people with whom you work. Brainstorming over video chat, updating each other on projects by text, sharing files over e-mail: In each scenario, the communication tool you're using functions as a simulated space where you meet to work together. Making this space work well poses a unique set of communication, scheduling, and motivational challenges.

What's *not* virtual, of course, is the person on the other end. The pixelated, jerky figures on your screen are flesh and blood, and your interactions with them are subject to the same dynamics as any other professional encounter. You need to build rapport and trust, communicate effectively, and be productive. But these goals can be harder to achieve in a virtual setting, when communication becomes muddled, scheduling grows more complicated, and isolation and distractions prey on your ability to stay focused and motivated.

This book shows you how to solve the technological and administrative puzzles of virtual collaboration; it presents solutions such as finding and using the right tools, routinizing communication, and tracking progress. And it gives you tips for managing the social and emotional experience, too, as you strive to deepen professional connections while working in isolation.

The challenges of virtual collaboration

Just because we're all working remotely at some point in our careers doesn't mean that we're good at it. The habits that helped you in an office won't always make sense when you're working remotely. Which changes are hardest to adapt to?

You must set and manage expectations more pro-actively. One of the great things about virtual work is that each person can tailor the arrangement to their own needs—and this means that everyone does it differently. There's no standard workday, no common conventions for writing text messages. And no one knows when it's their turn to speak on a conference call.

You are your own IT department. If you're in an office, you can rely on IT specialists to address your technology issues. But if you're off-site, you need to get up and running—and stay there—even if it's not your area of expertise.

You spend more time building and maintaining relationships. When there are fewer chance encounters, you must purposefully and proactively reach out to colleagues. Because every interaction requires some planning, it carries a higher tax—more e-mails to answer, more calendar notifications to sort. Yet the social distance between you and your colleagues is harder to close—some days you feel so lonely you wind up talking the ear off the delivery person.

You're communicating with blunt tools. Without face-to-face interaction, you spend more time sussing out unspoken expectations, trying to interpret incomplete messages, or sifting through pages of project updates.

Other people can't "see" your work. How do you let colleagues know you're not binge-viewing the latest hit series? How can you manage people's perceptions of you with such limited opportunities for meaningful interaction?

To meet these challenges, you'll need great communication skills and a sense of initiative. You'll develop new instincts for how to express courtesy, enthusiasm, or dissent in digital communication. You'll become more self-reliant as solving technological glitches becomes routine, and more self-motivated as you develop rhythms with both your work and your partners to get your job done. You'll also learn to tolerate the ambiguity inherent in this work—to find the humor and spirit in a coworker's terse e-mails or to make a decision on your own when your colleagues aren't around for consultation.

For you, the payoff is a kind of flexibility that's hard to come by in a traditional office. Virtual collaboration gives you more control over your day-to-day experience and frees you to do work in the time, place, and manner that best suits your needs. And flexibility for *you* can actually mean a closer working relationship with each of your colleagues, whether they're a onetime collaborator in another city or a regular coworker who sits next to you in the office four days out of five. You'll stay in touch even when normal, side-by-side routines don't bind you together, and you'll keep assignments moving along so that everyone stays productive.

This level of productivity, of course, requires some up-front investment in relationship basics. You'll start at the ground level by setting expectations with your collaborators about how you'll work together.

Clarify Expectations for Your Work

Clarify Expectations
for Your Work

You and a colleague across the country have agreed: You'll draft the proposal that's due Monday, and they'll edit it. But as you start your work, you realize that there are details you're not sure about. Will you run an outline by them before you start writing? Does editing mean they'll insert commas and remove typos, or does it involve substantive changes to content and language? Will they input the edits directly onto the draft or deliver comments over the phone? If they text you at nine p.m. on Sunday with a question, are you supposed to answer right away? Most of these questions are easily reconciled if you're working in close proximity—you can ask for clarification in passing or have your colleague look at something odd on your screen.

But the flexibility of remote work means that you and your colleagues might be operating under vastly different circumstances—even in different time zones. What's convenient or natural for you might not be the same for them. If you're working from home in a pinch and don't set expectations with your colleagues in the office, they may forget, for example, that you're off-site and unable to keep physical design sketches circulating. In this chapter, you'll learn how to establish the scope of your collaboration and institute rules that will help you succeed.

Define the work

Whether you're completing a onetime project for a client or collaborating on a monthly corporate update, delineating the work is one of the most important conversations you'll have with your virtual partners. How will you describe your common goals? What milestones will you set for the work? What form will your deliverables take? Getting alignment on these questions smooths the way for your work together and makes all of you mutually responsible.

Start by initiating a discussion with your colleagues with the explicit goal of talking about how you'll collaborate effectively. To avoid having a long conversation about process over e-mail or phone, for bigger projects draft a collaboration charter—a shared document that everyone in the group can access and edit. (See the sidebar "Virtual Collaboration Charter.") Ask the person leading the project to circulate this template. Or if there's no designated leader or the work is ongoing and not related to a singular project, create your own template and invite others to edit it. Push your collaborators to contribute to the charter from their own areas of expertise—for example, the person responsible for each milestone should help set target dates. Then schedule a call to review the document together, resolving disagreements and answering questions.

At the end of the call, ask everyone to verbally sign off, and keep a copy in an accessible location—your Dropbox folder, for example—so that people can refer to the document thereafter. With this collaboration charter, everyone has a common reference they can turn to for basic questions while they're out in the field ("Is this client request in scope?") or simply out of touch ("Am I supposed to have this assignment ready on the fifth or the fifteenth?"). And if the communication hurdles of your arrangement lead to misunderstandings down the line, you'll use this document to resolve disagreements and maintain accountability.

If you can't orchestrate a conversation such as this with the whole team, or if you're not part of one, create a charter for yourself. Schedule a one-on-one phone or video conversation with your boss, or set

VIRTUAL COLLABORATION CHARTER

Include the following elements in your collaboration charter:

- *Goals.* What is the desired outcome of our work together? For example: "We'll deliver a global marketing plan for a new product to our client."

- *Scope.* What are our high-level deliverables or performance targets? What lies outside our scope? For example, "Deliverables are a written plan (20 pages) and slide presentation over video chat (one hour). Design content is outside the scope."

- *Resources.* What resources—financial, human, and so on—do we have to work with? For long-term or ongoing collaborations, how do we expect our resources to evolve? For example,

(continued)

VIRTUAL COLLABORATION CHARTER

"The client has sent a PDF with market research from the developers and has made its R&D staff available. Our teams in India, Japan, and London will contribute input from their markets."

- *Schedule boundaries.* What are the major constraints on our schedule? Do we need to plan for time-zone differences? For example, "The client is planning a campaign launch on August 1. In June, we're ramping up a new project with another client in a different city."

- *Milestones.* How will we benchmark our progress? For example, "Approved design by March 1. Contract with vendor signed by March 15. Prototype from vendor by April 15."

aside a quiet hour for the work. Take notes, and share the document with the people you work with most frequently: It will come in handy if confusion or conflict develops later on.

For short-term gigs, where a formal charter doesn't make sense, run through these questions in an informal conversation with the colleagues who might be affected by your absence. If you're working from home for a week while the office moves, for example, talk to your supervisor before you leave. The following types of questions help clarify the work:

- "What are our goals for this work over the next week? Here's what I have planned . . ."

- "What deliverables would you like to see by the time we're back? What can wait? So far I'm thinking . . ."

- "What resources will I have while I'm out of the office? I need . . ."

- "Are there any schedule issues I should plan for? I already know about . . ."

- "What milestones should we set over the next week? By Wednesday, I'd like to have done . . ."

Agree on roles, tasks, and processes

Now that you're clear about what work needs to be done, who will complete which tasks? Coordinating roles and responsibilities is inherently more challenging when you're not in the same physical location. If you don't check in frequently, your colleague in Cape Town will lose track of what your teammate in Miami is doing. But sending multiple messages to multiple recipients on multiple channels can create confusion and make it hard to track progress. To organize who does what, take the following steps:

- *Simplify the work.* Streamline things as much as you can, and agree on who ultimately owns each task. If you aren't in a position to influence these decisions, talk one-on-one with the people you'll be working with most directly to make sure that you're all on the same page. If necessary, press your boss for more direction—and suggest the changes you'd like to see.

- *Have each person share a "role card."* Itemize important information such as the person's title, general responsibilities, work schedule, close collaborators, and the key tasks, decisions, deliverables, and milestones the individual is attached to. These "cards" could be individual documents, e-mails, or entries on a shared wiki or message board. Review the info briefly during a meeting to clear up any misunderstandings.

- *Agree on protocols.* Guidelines are needed for important activities such as group decisions, tracking progress, and sharing updates. Consider these questions: "Who in the group needs to be involved in each of these activities?" and "Which communication technologies will you use for each of these activities?" If you lack the authority to lead this conversation, pose these questions to your supervisor with respect to yourself: "What activities do *I* need to be involved in? I'm thinking . . ." or "How should I share updates during a meeting? I'd like to . . ."

Establish a code of conduct

When you're out of the office, you're free to structure your time to suit your own particular habits and needs. But the routines that work for you also need to work for your colleagues. Set healthy boundaries, and establish a code of conduct to which you can hold yourself accountable. And if you're out of the office just for the short term, managing your colleague's expectations matters even more, since they're

TABLE 1

Planning for professionalism: establishing a code of conduct with your colleagues

Here are some questions to spark a discussion with your colleagues about how you'll work together. Asking close collaborators these questions, and supplying your answers for others, will help you avoid confusion. There are additional questions to pose to your boss, to gain clarity for their expectations of you.

Topic	Question
For everyone	
Hours	• How many hours each day or week will you work when you're not in the office? What times of the day are you expected to be available?
	• If you're in different time zones, how will you schedule meetings to accommodate one another?
	• Will you have visibility into each other's schedules (perhaps through an e-mail client such as Outlook) or create a shared team schedule (such as a Google calendar)?
Delegation and cooperation	• Do you have the authority to assign work to colleagues, and vice versa?
	• What responsibility do you have to accept a coworker's request for help? What freedom do you have to politely refuse?
	• What kind of help is each collaborator willing and eager to give? What is out of bounds?
	• How much lead time should you give a colleague when you make a request?

(continued)

TABLE 1 (*continued*)

Topic	Question
For everyone	
Etiquette	• What kind of confidentiality or privacy will your communications be subject to?
	• What steps should you take to redirect e-mails or phone calls when you're on vacation or when your regular hours change?
The unexpected	• Can you plan for times when you'll have to deviate from these rules (for example, holidays, busy seasons, maternity leave)?
	• Can anyone cover for you in case of emergency?
For your boss	
General	• How much independence will I have?
	• What resources will be available to me to complete my work?
	• How much will I be expected to travel?
Delegation and cooperation	• Do I have the authority to assign work to colleagues, and vice versa?
	• What responsibility do I have to accept a co-worker's request for help? What freedom do I have to politely refuse?

used to your regular schedule and routine. Flagging a situation that's out of the ordinary ("Working from home on Wednesday; back in the office on Thursday") will allow your work to continue without interruption.

If you're part of a team, ask your leader to clarify the terms of engagement. If you're an independent contributor, initiate this conversation yourself with your colleagues. Table 1 outlines the topics to cover in each conversation.

Shared expectations go a long way toward easing the frictions that exist in every working relationship. But whether you can meet these expectations as a remote partner largely depends not on your good intentions or memory, but on your technology. In the next chapter, you'll learn how to find and use the tools you need to be a reliable contributor.

Manage Your Technology

Manage Your Technology

When you work outside a traditional office, connectivity is everything. If your internet fails in the middle of a meeting, you can waste precious minutes on hold with customer support while your window of overlap with a colleague closes.

It's frustrating to spend time problem-solving issues that don't fall within your area of expertise, but the stakes are high. Missed deadlines, canceled appointments, botched handoffs: Technical glitches can scuttle your work and create frustration among your peers. At some point, "technical difficulties" start looking like old-fashioned irresponsibility. So how do you anticipate and resolve your technical problems before they become problems for your colleagues, too?

Your responsibilities will depend on the nature of your collaboration. If you're a full-time employee with a regular or permanent remote-work gig, your IT department will help you select and set up tools and even troubleshoot problems. But if you don't have the benefit of IT support, these guidelines will help you get your technology up and running on your own.

Assess your needs

What tools do you need to get your work done? Which will help you collaborate most effectively with others? The answers to these questions aren't always the same. For example, you might prefer legacy software that other people don't know how to use. Or maybe your colleague likes working through problems on Slack, but you'd rather talk than type your way through complicated issues. To determine which technologies will make the relationship work best from *both* ends, take an inventory of your own needs and those of your collaborator.

You'll start, of course, with a lightweight laptop or tablet. But what else? Do you trade large audio or video files with each other? Do you prefer instant messaging (IM) to long-form e-mails? Use the following questions to organize your thoughts:

- What's your primary way of communicating—phone, e-mail, or some other channel?

- Do you hold meetings? If so, how?

- Do you need any specialized software or hardware?

- Do you need to access any databases?

- How do you store and synchronize content? How important is it to your work that you see and share real-time updates to files, data, and the like?

- How much storage capacity do you need?

- What precautions do you take to secure information?

- What activities do you need to do on your mobile phone?

- Do you share or synchronize calendars?

- Do you need project-management or issue-tracking software (such as Asana, Smart-sheet, SharePoint, JIRA, Microsoft Project, or Basecamp)?

- What compatibilities must you plan for—for example, Apple versus Android?

You don't have to answer these questions on your own: Talk about them with your colleagues, too. As you're making your final selections, consider these additional questions:

- If you work for a company, what technology does it provide?

- Do you have access to an IT department? If not, can your coworkers recommend a private consulting service?

- What's your budget for all technology—purchase, installation, and maintenance? Will your company pay for any of this?

- What assistance can your company provide? For example, does it offer free copies of software or virtual training?

- Are the tools you plan to use easy to install, learn, and use? Are they reliable?

- Do the tools require you to acquire any new components?

Select your hardware and software

With the information you've gathered from your boss and your colleagues, you're ready to choose your tools. Sometimes these decisions, at least the big ones, will be made by a team leader or by IT; in other cases, it's up to you.

Hardware

When it comes to hardware, determining what you need, beyond your mobile phone and laptop or tablet, depends on where you work. Are you putting together a home office? Are you packing a bag for a work trip? Do you need materials you can travel with every day to a coworking space or a client site? Focus on the items that matter most to your setup, including the following:

- *A good internet provider.* For everything from communicating to uploading and downloading files. Pay attention to the results of your inter-net speed tests: For most types of work, 25 to 50 Mbps download speed and 10 Mbps upload speed should be sufficient.

- *A landline.* For high-quality audio during a conversation. Consider installing one in a home office, and plan for access when you travel.

- *Your own hotspot.* For supplying a backup Wi-Fi connection anywhere. Look for tools that are super portable, such as a USB stick from your wireless provider or your mobile phone.

- *A headset.* For lengthy, hands-free conversa-tions. Look for a wired version that you won't have to charge or pair wirelessly with your phone or computer.

- *A mini power strip.* For securing a power supply when you're out and about, especially in a crowded café or at a convention. If all the

outlets are taken, ask one claimant to plug into
your strip instead. Look for a compact, cordless
model.

- *Extra cables.* For moving your work easily,
  without the rigmarole of unplugging every
  component.

- *Cable case.* For organizing and transporting
  cables. Look for something with compart-
  ments, for tangle-free cords and easy sorting
  of adapters.

- *Battery and car adapter.* For charging your devices on the go. Look for an inverter (it changes
  DC to AC) so that you can charge your laptop in
  your car.

- *Labels and tags.* For keeping track of your stuff
  so that your laptop, tablet, charger, headset,
  and so on, don't get mixed up with someone
  else's—even in your own home. Look for color-
  ful cable IDs, stickers, or asset tags.

Software

With software, what's right for you depends on the kind of work you'll be doing. Are you collaborating on a process or creating separate components for a final product? Do you work primarily with words, images, or audio? Focus on the items that matter most to the tasks you'll be completing, such as the following:

- *Document collaboration.* Look for tools that let you edit in real time and share files that are too large for e-mail. Examples: Google Drive, Dropbox.

- *Note sharing.* Look for tools that collect all your notes and clippings in one place, sync across devices, and allow you to share content with colleagues. Examples: Evernote, Simplenote, Google Docs.

- *Scheduling.* Look for tools that let you manage joint calendars with colleagues, and set up in your own calendar various appointment slots that others can sign up for. Examples: Google Calendar, Calendly.

- *Screen sharing.* Look for tools that let you share with multiple users at the same time. Prioritize speed and reliability over complicated features. Examples: join.me, Skype, WebEx, Google Hangouts.

- *Instant messaging.* Look for tools that you can connect to your phone, laptop, and tablet. Example: Slack, Google Chat, HipChat.

Don't be afraid of trying out new tools, but the conservative choice is often the best. Pick items that are simple, reliable, and easy to use, maintain, and replace. So much the better if you already own them: Using familiar technology will save you time and keep your costs low.

Put your tools to work

If you're part of a team, ideally your team leader will coordinate a conversation around how you'll use the tools that you've identified. If you're working in a looser arrangement, it probably doesn't make sense to work out detailed rules, but you can still take the lead to clarify a few key items:

❑ *Venue.* Which interactions belong on the phone, in e-mail, and so on?

❑ *Availability.* How responsive will you be on each of these tools? How will you get in touch if something's truly urgent?

❑ *Meetings.* Who will set up and lead conference calls or host video chats? How will you get the call-in number and handouts in advance? If you're the only person calling in, who will introduce you? If the whole meeting is virtual, how will all of you identify yourselves when you speak?

❑ *Version control.* How will you make sure that you and your colleagues are working efficiently and without redundancy? When something goes wrong, who will be responsible for fixing the problem?

❑ *Coordination.* Which materials or tools do you need to synchronize? Who will set up and manage shared technologies?

❑ *Sensitive material.* How will you safely share and store sensitive or proprietary material?

❑ *Politeness and privacy.* What does good behavior look like with each of these technologies? For example, can you call a colleague without an appointment? How will you avoid interrupting each other on a video chat if there's a delay?

You don't need a hard-and-fast rule for everything: Pick the issues that matter most to your work experience or that seem to be troublesome for your coworkers. Bring up the topic in a respectful, upbeat way, and focus on a short list of specific behaviors. If your colleagues aren't responsive to your suggestions, or if you feel uncomfortable talking to them about it, focus on disciplining your own tech use. Can you ask for handouts before a meeting? Redirect coworkers to your preferred communication tool? Update your IM status to let people know you're too busy to answer calls right now? Be proactive and consistent, and others may follow your lead.

What to do when technology fails

Technology failures are confusing and embarrassing. But you can reduce their impact by accepting that they'll happen sooner or later and by planning for them.

Prepare, test, and practice. Master critical trouble-shooting moves before you need them. For example, know how to recover lost files and remember rebooting your computer sometimes resolves issues. When you're first setting up your remote work tools—before a big conference call—conduct a premortem to catalog potential risks and to play out worst-case scenarios. Brainstorm plan Bs (for example, what should you do if you're kicked off the call?), and do a few trial runs to make sure they're viable. Keep a physical copy of a *crisis card* close at hand with information such as your account number with an internet service provider and the contact information for a local, in-home IT service (see the sidebar "Technology Crisis Card").

Use the buddy system. A designated colleague can help you solve tech problems on the fly and act as a liaison for you with the rest of the team while your system is down. You can text them while your machine reboots, or e-mail them as you dial in again

TECHNOLOGY CRISIS CARD

Keep this basic information on hand (in hard copy) for when things go wrong:

- Name of your internet service provider and a help-line phone number

- Name of the account holder and your account number

- Account information for your most important tools (the e-mail address or name that the tool is registered under, password hints, security questions, purchase information)

- Name and version of your computer's current operating system

- Name and phone number of an in-home IT service

after a dropped call. Don't wait for disaster to strike before you establish this relationship: Ask a collaborator ahead of time, and agree on the communication channels you'll use.

Learn from others. Augment your own know-how with tips from your coworkers. If you're part of a virtual team, ask your leader to circulate a memo with recommended plan Bs, resources, help links, and contact information. Or reach out informally on your own to colleagues: "What backup plans do you have in place if your tech setup fails? Any advice for me?" Consider creating a shared document where people can post their suggestions, or start a dedicated thread in a group discussion board or another forum. If you get good feedback, print it out and keep it handy offline.

Managing your own technology will sometimes feel like a strange addendum to your "real" job. But your professional reputation depends on your competence in this realm. If your colleagues can count on you to upload files correctly, they're much more likely to trust you with the bigger things. In the next chapter, you'll learn additional best practices for creating trusting, productive relationships with your coworkers.

Build Productive Relationships

Build Productive Relationships

All the shared documents in the world won't help you if your coworkers don't trust you. Maybe they don't think you'll be available if they need to reach you, or they don't lobby for your name to be thrown out for consideration when a team is forming to work on a new product. Perhaps they're constantly nagging you: "Any update since the last time I asked (thirty minutes ago)?"

The success of your collaboration comes down to the relationships you've created—relationships that exist, in part or in total, on phone lines and through satellite signals. In this chapter, you'll learn to establish and maintain rapport, credibility, and true mutual respect from a distance.

"Meet" your colleagues

If you're working remotely for the short term, you probably know all your collaborators. But if you haven't met everyone in person, begin with a little background research. Google, LinkedIn, Facebook, and Twitter are obvious starting points, but think about your personal contacts, too. Do you know anyone who's worked with this person or could speak to their reputation? Ask around, in a positive way: "I'm excited to start working with Nita! What was your experience with her?"

Ideally, you'd meet any new coworker face to face, but that's not always possible. So imitate an in-person meeting as closely as you can: Video chat is best, followed by phone as a distant second. E-mail is your last resort. The more information available to you (facial expressions, gestures, vocal tone), the better you can interpret communications from this person later on.

Initiate a get-to-know-you conversation in person or online. Pose these questions to any colleague, but focus on the people you expect to work with most closely:

- Where are they based? Are they also navigating remote work?

- What's their professional background? Their current role?

- How are they approaching your joint work, and what information do they have that you don't—about the project, the client, your organization?

- What prospects for the work excite them?

- What risks are they worried about?

- What are their expectations about how you'll collaborate?

- Which communication tools do they like to use, and which do they dislike?

- Do they have any major constraints you should know about, such as a deadline for another project?

- What percentage of their time are they devoting to this project?

- If they work for a different organization, how would they describe its collaborative culture?

At the end of the conversation, schedule your next interaction. Follow up on a particular issue, or make a plan to chat again (set a specific time).

Establish trust

As in face-to-face relationships, trust in a virtual context requires transparency—about what you know, what you want, and what you're able to do. But these signals are harder to read, because of the social distance that virtual communication technologies create. So they need a boost. Let's look at how to help establish trust with your colleagues.

Make the most of "swift trust." Genuine rapport develops slowly, but people usually feel a surge of friendliness and goodwill when a group first forms. Reinforce perceptions of your credibility by beating deadlines, and be generous with praise or gratitude, especially in writing.

Be predictable. Keep regular hours, and schedule check-in calls at the same time every day or week. Respond to e-mails, texts, calls, and the like, in a routine way, even if only to say you'll answer later. If you only work out of the office occasionally, try to establish a set day that you do so. If you can't predict which day you'll be out, communicate the time as soon as you know, and be explicit about when and how folks should get in touch with you. Setting accurate expectations is more important than sending the message that you're always open for business.

Be persistent. Don't assume that because interacting online feels awkward at first, the relationship is doomed to fail. Keep smiling, and keep looking for opportunities to make a personal connection with your coworkers. What starts out as stilted ("You had a peanut butter sandwich for lunch? So did I.") might turn into a genuine exchange or at least a humorous point of reference.

Manage conflict

Conflict that erupts over screens is not much different from in-person fights: It centers on tasks ("I don't agree with you about how to do the work") or interpersonal relationships ("I don't like you"), and without quick intervention, the one can quickly turn into the other. But because communicating online is confusing to begin with, and because it disinhibits antisocial behavior, you'll want to be especially pro-active in confronting disagreements before they turn bad. The following dos and don'ts can help you have more productive interactions.

Do

- Discuss interpersonal conflicts in person, if possible. If you can't, use video chat or a phone call, and ask a supervisor to mediate.

- Pursue task-related arguments. If you don't agree with a plan of action or if you have a problem with someone's work, speak up.

- Take your problems to a dedicated problem-solving venue, such as a troubleshooting thread on a discussion board, a one-on-one call, or an "ongoing issues" agenda item during a meeting.

- Switch venues—from e-mail to phone, for example—when you can't resolve a disagreement easily.

- Practice active listening. Since communication technologies limit visual and vocal cues, check your understanding by reflecting back what you see and hear. See the sidebar "Scripts for Conflict" for more tips on how to conduct these conversations.

Don't

- Don't try to resolve complicated or personal disagreements over e-mail.

- Don't wait for task-related arguments to turn personal.

- Don't blindside people or embarrass them in front of their peers. If someone thinks you aren't treating them fairly, they won't react well.

- Don't be afraid to ask for a reassignment. If you're involved in an intractable conflict, look for ways to redistribute tasks so that your interpersonal problems don't affect the work.

Building strong relationships with colleagues whom you don't see every day requires persistence, empathy, and a genuine interest in the person behind the machine. To express these traits successfully, you'll need something else, too: strong communication skills across a variety of platforms.

SCRIPTS FOR CONFLICT

When you confront a colleague about a problem at work, you'll often discover motivations and interests that differ from yours. These conversations require a lot of back-and-forth, so schedule a phone call or video chat. Let them know ahead of time what you want to discuss, so they can prepare, too. Take notes while you talk, in Google Docs or some other place you both can see and edit. Then dive in with some of these questions:

Understanding your differences

- "I'm sensing a gap in how we think about _____. What's going on there?"

- "You seem concerned about _____. Can you help me understand what's driving that?"

- "I'm concerned about _____, but you don't seem to be. Can you help me understand why not?"

- "How does our shared work fit in with your other priorities right now?"

- "I see the main purpose of this work as ____. What about you?"

- "The outcome I'm most excited about from this work is ____. What about you?"

- "The ____ aspect of this work is the most challenging for me right now [or is taking the most time]. What about you?"

Reconciling your differences

- "In an ideal world, how would you like this to go?"

- "In an ideal world, I'd like ____ to happen. Is that possible?"

(continued)

SCRIPTS FOR CONFLICT

- "I would most like to see you take _____ action. Can you do that? If not, what do you propose?"

- "What action would you most like to see from me?"

- "I think we have a lot of common ground around _____ [name the goal, task, problem, or outcome]. Let's start by figuring out how we want that to go."

- "I'm really glad to learn about _____ [motivation, goal, or problem] that you have. I think I can contribute there . . ."

- "I see _____ [motivation, goal, or problem] that you have as being connected to _____ priority that I have. How can we build on that?"

- "It sounds like _____ [task] is more relevant to you, and _____ [task] to me—want to trade?"

Specificity is the key to this kind of conversation. Isolate the behaviors you'd like them to change, and keep the list short, say, one to three items. Propose only things you think are important and doable, and look for opportunities for reciprocity.

Communicate
Effectively

Communicate Effectively

C ommunicating with virtual colleagues can feel like screaming into the wind. It takes much effort, but you're still not sure you're being heard. Because you're not face to face, you won't see the glints of recognition in their eyes when your idea lands, or catch the skeptical looks on their faces. You could spend all day replying to e-mails, and still miss a coworker's SOS if you're not also regularly checking texts, calls, IMs, and all the rest of the dozen other channels you use to communicate. How are you supposed to get any work done when just staying in touch requires so much time?

In this chapter, you'll learn how to get the most out of your technology, capture your colleagues' attention, and limit the total amount of time you spend on it.

Pick the right channel

You've spent two weeks trying to get a video call on the calendar with a busy colleague, but when the moment comes, you realize with embarrassment that the only thing you really have to ask is a simple yes-or-no question. Five minutes into the call, your colleague asks you in a disbelieving tone, "So . . . that's it?"

Anyone who's made this mistake knows how important it is to match the mode of communication with the content. If the fit is off, you'll waste time and goodwill on fruitless or confusing interactions. Written formats strip emotional context and inhibit back-and-forth on complicated or extended points. Audio and video can be intrusive and often require advance planning. With too many participants in any one of these, it can also be difficult to follow the thread of who says what.

How can you make an exchange as effective and efficient as possible? To decide which mode to use, ask yourself two questions. First, what do you want the recipient to do after you convey your message? If you think they'll have a lot of questions or will need to craft a detailed reply, phone or video is best. If you just need a quick answer, try e-mail, text, or another IM service.

Second, how do you think the recipient will react after you convey your message? If you think they're likely to be confused or upset or to have any other heightened emotional response, go for video or phone, where you can project and read feelings more accurately.

There are other considerations, too. If the message is urgent, tools that let you reach people instantly—like text, IM, or phone—are best. If it's complex, then

BRIDGE TIME ZONES

Try these tips for communicating with colleagues in different places:

- Get some real-time face time, even with colleagues in different time zones. Don't let the logistics put you off: If you can't find a mutually convenient hour, be the one to compromise.

- Find a shared window of time in your working days, and make sure you're regularly available during that period.

- If you don't have any available hours in common, talk explicitly about how you'll manage trading any necessary information to keep things moving. What do each of you need from the other to get your work done?

phone, video, or a shared document is best. You also need to think about the audience: to get input from multiple people, use phone, video, or a group messaging service such as Slack; for one-on-one or unidirectional communications, e-mail and text are OK. For tips on handling time zones and language barriers across these platforms, see the sidebars "Bridge Time Zones" and "Surmount Language and Cultural Barriers."

As you get a feel for what works best with your particular colleagues, remember that you can always switch between channels. Just because a conversation starts on e-mail doesn't mean it has to stay there. If you feel as if the discussion is becoming unproductive, consider whether a change in venue could help: "It's hard to answer that question over text—can I call you?"

SURMOUNT LANGUAGE AND CULTURAL BARRIERS

If you're working with people in different countries or cultures, you can close the gaps in several ways:

- *Ask them how they prefer to communicate.* You'd do this with any colleague, but put extra thought into it when you and your coworkers aren't fluent in the same languages. Are they more comfortable with written or oral communications? Does the topic make a difference in how they like to communicate—for example, a highly technical point versus a general status update? Consider how cultural norms might interact with the technologies you choose, too, especially when you need to work through a disagreement or discuss a sensitive issue.

- *Build on common ground.* However different your and your colleague's past experiences, you do share something right now: this work. Are you both sticklers about punctuality? Do you geek out about the same things? Are both of you having trouble getting a certain tool to function properly?

- *Do your own research.* If you're working with more than one person who lives in a different country or if you will be collaborating with someone for a long time, read up about the area. Learn about their cultures and traditions. Occasionally check in with the main source of news for that area, or find related and reliable sources to follow on Twitter. Express your interest in learning more, and ask your colleagues directly for their recommendations.

Get—and keep—your colleagues' attention over e-mail

Whether you're scheduling a meeting, sharing information, or making a request, most interactions with your virtual collaborators begin with an e-mail. When colleagues see your name in their inbox, you want them to think, "I'd better see what that's about!" Frame your message for maximum impact by following several practices.

Craft your subject line carefully. Clarity and brevity rule. Use the project name, or set expectations ("Quick question" or "Project update: reply by COB [close of business]").

Lead with what you want. Don't make them skim to the bottom of an e-mail or suffer through a meandering voicemail to find out what you're asking. Start with a clear request: "I'd like your help organizing the permissions for our upcoming showcase. I've drafted a timeline—can you review it and let me know by the end of the week?"

Provide context. What do they need to know for this request to click? How does it connect to their bigger picture? Are there recent events that help explain what you're asking for—complications, setbacks, errors?

Spell out your request. What specific actions do you want the recipient to take? If you need a response immediately, don't assume they'll get back to you in a timely manner. And if you want an update later on how things are going, make that explicit, too.

Make it memorable. Use powerful, vivid language. Avoid exaggerations or rhetorical flights of fancy: Short sentences with forceful, simple verbs make a strong impression.

Curb emoji usage. Emoji can effectively convey emotion, but they can also make you look immature or out of touch. Do you have a relationship with the recipient that will help them interpret the signal correctly?

Say thank you. It's common sense, but not always common practice: Gratitude oils the gears of all working relationships. Don't ask "Please?" without saying thank you.

End with a call to action. Refocus their attention on your central objective: the task you want them to perform, attached to a specific timeline. "Today I need last quarter's numbers for the Bhattacharya account, and tomorrow I'll follow up about the Meyer and Abbott accounts."

Hold people accountable

Maintaining accountability with virtual collaborators requires empathy and ingenuity. As in other parts of real life, it's a good idea to start by reflecting on where a recalcitrant colleague is coming from. What are their motivations, interests, and constraints? If both of you are part of a team, take into account the other person's role on the team and the chain of command. Who are they responsible to, and how does your collaborative work align with their role?

If you're working together in a looser arrangement, pose this question more broadly: What's at stake for them here? How can you connect your issue to the things they already care about? Once you have a handle on the answers to these questions, you can try several communication strategies.

Push colleagues to commit to concrete plans. A concrete plan is an action item plus a deadline. If you keep hearing "I'll get to that soon," be blunt: "When? How about Monday?" Document your agreement in writing, then remind them of the commitment as the deadline approaches. By extracting an explicit promise from them, you take away their plausible deniability for ignoring your texts and calls come Monday.

Let them know they have an audience. The biggest leverage you have in this situation is probably your overlapping professional networks. You can't hail them in their cubicle with a hearty "Did you get my e-mail?" while the rest of the office listens in, but you can remind them that other people will see their work. Bring it up in a positive way: "Dan and I were just talking about this project—he's excited about our work and asked us to share the finished product!" Your collaborators will understand that you aren't the only person with high expectations for their performance. If you need to push harder, express concern before anger, and remember that a threat is never professional (and rarely productive, anyway).

Create a sense of reciprocity. If your request is one-way, they might think of it as a favor. Push back against this illusion by showing that you're in a mutual professional relationship, where both people are giving and receiving something of value:

- Surpass their expectations by beating deadlines and exceeding quality standards in your work.

- Volunteer to help them with an annoying or difficult task.

- Ask them what they want! "I'm so grateful for the work you're doing on this. What can I do to make this a good experience [or investment of time] for you?"

- Deepen the social dimension of the relationship. What are they looking forward to this weekend? Is their pet recovering from its recent surgery?

- For a long-term assignment or a particularly onerous task, send them a small gift. An ebullient thank you is a great motivator, and while you can't beguile a faraway coworker with homemade cookies, you can have flowers delivered to their desk.

Maintain a positive, generous frame of mind. Your grievances may be legitimate, but grousing about them will only poison the relationship further. Interpret their communications with charity, and make kind assumptions.

Give and receive feedback

Generosity is particularly valuable when it comes to feedback. You might struggle to figure out when and how to deliver constructive criticism in a virtual setting—and receiving it can be just as challenging. "Your recent work contained some major problems" looks much worse in an e-mail than it sounds when delivered with a compassionate facial expression by someone you frequently lunch with.

To start the conversation off well, pick your timing carefully. Avoid delivering difficult information right before another meeting or a deadline they have. If you're using video, position the camera at eye level so you're not looming over your interlocutor. Keep your body language open and relaxed, and maintain natural eye contact.

Plot out the actual conversation ahead of time, following these steps:

1. *Think about the bigger picture.* What else is going on in this person's personal and professional life right now? Sometimes that's harder to know when you aren't interacting in person every day—but see if you can find out. Also,

what's the context for this feedback in your relationship with them? What do you want this feedback to accomplish in the relationship?

2. *Start on a high note.* Be warm, and don't skip the usual small talk. Emotion is harder to read over video or on the phone, so be explicit about your positive feelings: "I'm really enjoying working with you." "We've still got some work to do, but I'm confident we'll get there."

3. *Express honest appreciation for the other person's work.* Start with some good feedback, and be specific. What are they doing well? What have they made easier or more interesting for you?

4. *Give feedback about a specific behavior.* Don't speculate about motives or talk about big patterns: Keep your comments concrete and narrowly focused to avoid a defensive

response. Listen to the reply, and follow up
on anything that seems ominous. For example,
if they won't meet your eyes, is it because of
where the camera is positioned, or do they
feel attacked?

5. *Suggest a specific fix, or ask them to come up
with one.* You want to end the conversation
with an action item for your colleague, something they feel ownership over and excitement
about. Ask how you can help them execute it.

6. *End on a positive note.* Thank them for listening to you, and reiterate the positive feedback
you gave at the beginning. Then follow up
with an e-mail briefly summarizing what you
agreed on, and thanking them again for the
conversation.

The key to giving effective feedback is do it right
away or to let your colleague know it's coming. If

you respond to all e-mails immediately with "Looks great!" it can be awkward to reach out later with a criticism, and you may miss the window of opportunity altogether. It's better to prepare meaningful comments immediately or to send a placeholder message: "Thanks for sharing! I'm planning to look at it Friday and will send you my feedback then."

Some of the same advice applies when you are on the receiving end of feedback. Ideally, the person contacting you shares your hierarchy of technologies and will reach out in person or by video or phone. If not, redirect the conversation: "I just got your e-mail about my performance on our last quarterly report. I'd like to talk more about this—could we do a video call tomorrow afternoon?" When the time comes, find a private location that's clear of distractions, and follow these tips:

1. *Prepare ahead of time.* Review your work and any previous feedback from your colleague/

supervisor. Reflect on how *you* think things are going.

2. *Listen, take notes, and ask questions.* Your first task isn't to respond to the criticism, but to understand it. What exactly are you being told, and do you understand the values or concerns behind it? Explain to your colleague that you're taking notes so you can review them later—otherwise they might think they don't have your full attention.

3. *Summarize the feedback verbally to check your understanding.* It's hard to process criticism under any circumstances, and technology generally increases people's emotional confusion. Repeat back key points: "I'm hearing that my humor on phone calls can be alienating and confusing to other people. Am I getting that right?"

4. *Clarify your emotions.* Part of professionalism is managing your feelings in difficult situations, so don't let video glitches or a delayed phone connection imply things about your response—own it openly: "This definitely comes as a surprise, and I'm sad to hear I've made people uncomfortable."

5. *Suggest a specific fix, or ask them to come up with one.* You want to end with an action item: What would solve this problem? Ask for help if you need it.

6. *Buy time.* If you don't feel you can respond well in the moment, end the conversation gracefully. "I think I need some time to process this feedback. Thank you for being open with me; can I follow up with you tomorrow?"

Working remotely can sometimes hinder people from offering you feedback, so ask for it. When you share your own work, invite comments explicitly and then follow up if you don't hear back. Because you're in another location, no one can casually stop you in the hallway to share their reaction. So be direct: "Nora, I think your ideas about the layout I sent last week would be really helpful. Can you take a look?"

Set boundaries

You want other people to reply to your e-mails and react to your work—but the influx of communications can be distracting. Think about the last time you were really in the zone during work. What brought you out of it? Was it your phone buzzing? An e-mail notification on your computer screen? Did a coworker try to strike up a conversation over IM, or did your boss send you a calendar request?

You don't get to choose when people interrupt you. But you *can* choose how to respond. And when you're bombarded by signals from your menagerie of communications devices, remember this: You don't have to answer everything immediately. Instead, create sensible schedule boundaries, and obey them.

For example, consider answering e-mails exclusively in the morning and again at the close of the day. In between, check in periodically to let people know you got their note: "Thanks for this message! I'll get back to you by the end of my day." Record a special voicemail greeting, or set up auto-reply messages for your e-mail for a couple hours. An anxious or peeved coworker who gets no response from you might assume that you're simply off the clock. A prompt, if not substantive, response will go a long way toward assuring them that you're just tied up with other work.

For text or IM conversations that go on too long, keep a rote response on hand:

- "This is interesting, and I want to talk more about it. I have to go now, but I'll message you to set up a call."

- "Thanks for these sharp comments; it's been helpful! Unfortunately, I have to go, but let's follow up later."

- "I'm glad you asked, but unfortunately now is not a good time for me—can you send me an e-mail?"

- "Let me get back to you this afternoon, when things settle down over here."

Finally, know when to bail. If you don't need to be involved in the discussion, don't be.

· · ·

Communicating effectively with your virtual colleagues requires imagination and discipline. You need to think strategically about how best to reach individual collaborators and push these interactions into the most productive channels—maybe without the help or even the awareness of your colleague. It's a lot to master, but the payoff will be worth the effort when you spend two hours each day on your inbox instead of four. Savings like these are the difference between feeling unproductive and feeling like a true contributor to the work at hand. You can enjoy more of the latter feeling by learning how to handle the most common challenges of remote work, in the following chapter.

Manage Common Problems

Manage Common Problems

Without the structure of office life, your schedule can easily devolve into anarchy. You have a meeting at 10 and a deadline at 5 . . . and everything else is up for grabs. How do you explain to your coworkers and friends that your nontraditional arrangement is still real *work*? How do you stay on task when your kids come home from school? You *can* get stuff done when no one is looking—and stay sane through it all.

Managing your workflow while keeping your own sense of well-being intact can be a tricky balance. To establish boundaries around your workday, you'll need to find ways of limiting unwanted intrusions from colleagues, friends, and family. But for your professional reputation as well as your own mental health, you'll need to stay connected to those very same people. This chapter will guide you through this seeming paradox, so that you can maximize your productivity—without compromising your happiness.

Set and maintain a schedule that works

As a virtual collaborator, you can theoretically work anywhere, anytime—except it's not that easy. It's not just a matter of discipline or self-control: You begin the day with the best of intentions, but life is disorderly and our brains crave distractions. Maybe you're getting a late start because the babysitter was delayed, or perhaps there's too much ambient noise in the airport lounge.

You can't make your babysitter punctual, but you *can* structure your own schedule to maximize your output while adapting to the natural patterns of daily life. The following best practices will help.

Have a workday. Whether you're working nine-to-five or overnight, setting and sticking to regular hours will help your brain focus and make you a more reliable collaborator. Your decision here depends on your working conditions—whether you need to keep the same hours that a home office keeps, overlap with colleagues on another continent, or be available for domestic life during certain hours. Experiment with these parameters to find the schedule that works best, and review the tips shared earlier in the section "Establish a code of conduct."

Develop a routine for getting started. The usual going-to-work drill (get up early, dress professionally, and so on) can help you get in the right frame of mind. Develop habits: Make coffee, walk the dog, go to the gym, clean out your e-mail inbox, review the work you did the day before, and so on.

Set realistic expectations about what you can accomplish each day. Build in time for breaks, distractions, logistics, and annoyances. Consider journaling how you spend your time for a few days, and use that log as a template going forward.

Chunk your day. Don't just work your way down a task list—plan how you'll use different parts of the day. For example, maybe you prefer to do writing-heavy work in the morning, leaving the afternoon open for interpersonal tasks. Be thoughtful about the sequencing, too. Which activities exhaust you, and which give you an energy boost? When are you at your best for phone calls, video chats, and in-person meetings? What do you need to get done before your colleague logs out for the day or before your kids come home? Remember to schedule breaks, too, since your brain needs downtime.

Moderate your time on the web. Being outside an office environment can make it harder to rein in how much time you spend clicking link to link when re-searching a colleague's question. Avoid sites you know are particularly dangerous to your focus. Experiment with briefly turning off your Wi-Fi to power through a difficult task.

Quit while you're ahead. Don't try to wrap up everything before you stop for the day. If you pause in the middle of something, you'll have an easier time getting back into the flow tomorrow.

Make your work visible to others

Many people still don't "get" remote work. Do you have a friend who doesn't understand why you can't meet for a two-hour lunch in the middle of the day if you're "just" working from home, or a colleague who thinks that "virtual collaborator" means you're MIA? Their (annoying) ideas about your work matter for three reasons. First, if they don't value your labor, they won't value your time. You'll be more vulnerable to interruptions from all sides. Second, it's demotivating when others don't recognize and respect your work. We all have a basic human need for affirmation, and work is no exception. Finally, if your colleagues don't believe you're working hard, they won't trust you. You'll watch your ideas get shortchanged and your responsibilities shrink.

So what can you do? Shape the perceptions of family, friends, colleagues, and clients—and manage the relationship when bad impressions persist—using a variety of strategies.

Stage your workspace. Select a location that projects the image you want to share with your colleagues. If you can, pick a background for your video calls that matches the look of your company's headquarters. Keep your desktop neat, and clear out nonwork detritus. Is the nude pencil-drawing behind your desk too much?

TIPS FOR PICKING A COWORKING SPACE

Finding too many distractions at home, and the local coffee shop too crowded? Consider a *coworking space*—a communal office that telecommuters or the self-employed pay a fee to use. A day pass or a regular membership gives you access to a mix of open space, offices, conference rooms, communications technology, and amenities such as a kitchen or a printer.

This arrangement unites many of the benefits of remote work with those of an office. People who use coworking spaces report that the lack of competition and office politics frees them to concentrate on what's meaningful about their work and to give and receive help in a purer spirit of collegiality. And working around other people gives them structure and motivation that's often absent at home, and a strong sense of community. The benefits are striking:

(continued)

TIPS FOR PICKING A COWORKING SPACE

Research shows that coworking spaces help people thrive at work at a high level, averaging 6 on a 7-point scale.

Whether you're using a coworking space, an airport lounge, or the corner coffee shop, here are some characteristics to look for:

- *Mixed seating.* Ideally, there would be desks *and* couches, cubicles *and* armchairs. Different setups are appropriate for different work activities. Can you get a change of scene and refresh your brain without leaving the venue?

- *Open and closed working spaces, with clear break areas.* Chance encounters with other people will feed your creativity and motivation, but you'll also want to protect yourself from unwanted intrusions. Does the space meet both needs?

- *A program of social and networking events.* If you're a regular at a coworking space, building personal and professional ties can act as a bulwark against some of the emotional challenges of remote work. Does the space facilitate these interactions?

What message does the tangle of winter coats and boots over your shoulder send to your colleagues? Set up a practice video chat with a friend who will tell you what your makeshift office really looks like. (If you're looking for workspace options other than a home office, see the sidebar "Tips for Picking a Coworking Space.")

Pay attention to your presentation. You want people to see you as a true professional, so give them some visual cues. If you're going to be on a video chat, dress as if you were going to an office. Look at the camera, lean forward with an attentive posture as you would at a real table, and don't multitask.

Above all, be thoughtful about how you talk about your arrangement. "I'm wearing my pj's and I haven't even taken a shower yet!" might be true, but your boss and colleagues don't need to know. It's OK to show your real life happening in the background, but make sure the foreground looks right, too. You *do* take what you're doing seriously—so make sure people can see that you do.

Focus on changing people's behavior, not opinions. You'd like your spouse to respect the fact that you're working, but right now you need them to hold their chore requests until you're off the clock. And you'd like your colleagues to stop joking about how you're on vacation while you work from home, but you need them to remember to credit you when they present to your boss.

Instead of having the whole "No, it's actually a *real job!*" conversation, make specific, actionable requests of other people, and keep enforcing your boundaries.

- With colleagues, say something along these lines: "I miss the headquarters sometimes, but this arrangement works best for me right now. By the way, I'd like to call in to your Friday meeting with the team." Or "Please copy me on e-mails about this topic from now on—it's part of my role."

- With your family, try this: "Let's talk about this when I'm done with work, in three hours." Or, "I'm still on the clock. Come find me at six."

Combat isolation

Working remotely often means working alone. You're constantly communicating, but sterile e-mail notifications and terse text messages can make you feel even more alienated. "Are you going to make the deadline?" and "See my corrections, attached here" don't resonate like a friendly smile.

Even when you're surrounded by people—at a coffee shop, in an airport lounge, at a makeshift desk on-site with a client—you may still miss the collegiality and sense of common purpose that an office provides. And you'll certainly miss the talk. When your neighbor casually asks, "How's it going?" you'll find you have a *lot* to say.

The downside of isolation isn't just emotional—it's tactical, too. You may not receive key information that made it around the office because no one remembered to share with you. It's frustrating and potentially damaging to your credibility to be left out like this. How many times are you willing to say to your boss, "What e-mail? I didn't get it," or "What error? No one told me about it," or "What deadline? It's not on my calendar."

Even if you love remote work, you don't want to be left out or left behind. So how can you adapt?

Be visible to your virtual colleagues. Let peers and supervisors know what you're doing, not just your accomplishments, but obstacles and works in progress. Add some social or personal content to the conversations, even if it feels weird at first. If you're having trouble establishing a rhythm, put your to-dos on a calendar. Send a daily round-up to your colleagues, such as a Monday morning greeting, with your agenda for the week. Ask them what's on tap for them for the week ahead. Try out different options, and see what your individual coworkers respond to best.

Invite casual contact (when you want it). When you're doing work that doesn't require a lot of focus, let your colleagues know that you're open to spontaneous interactions. Broadcast your status over Twitter or Facebook, or customize your IM or Skype message: "My door is open this morning! Feel free to reach out if you want to follow up on something or just check in."

Stay connected to people in your physical location. Being around other people is essential to your well-being, so schedule regular face time. Friends, family, yoga buddies, local colleagues—cast as wide a net as you can, wherever you are. Put your plans on the calendar, and don't let work encroach too far on them.

Make time during the workday for restorative activities. The time you spend alone doesn't have to be cheerless. When you take a break, choose activities that you enjoy: Prepare and eat a good meal, visit your gym, check in with someone you love, listen to music, read or watch something you enjoy. Don't limit yourself to the erudite or dignified, either—have a mini dance party, check your fantasy sports team, or take a short nap. As long as you return to work feeling energized and refreshed, you're doing it right.

Commiserate. As you cycle through the natural lows and highs, the best thing you can do is talk about it, especially with your coworkers. Loneliness isn't shameful—for all you know, your colleague is going through the same thing.

. . .

There are a million ways to be a successful virtual collaborator. With diligence and some experimentation, you'll find the way that's right for you. Sometimes you'll hit your stride and feel like you've really mastered this way of working—and other times you'll find yourself neck-deep in e-mails, wondering how you'll ever get the hang of it. That's OK: As you become more comfortable and confident in your situation, the good periods will lengthen and the bad ones will shrink. Instead of dreading new tools, you'll be thrilled to figure out how they can solve a problem or augment a relationship. As you find better ways to plan your schedule, you may find that you have more time than ever before—and that you're more productive, too. And relationships that used to feel remote or awkward will gradually become collegial and, perhaps, will blossom into true friendship.

Learn More

Quick hits

Johnson, Whitney. "Collaboration Is Risky. Now, Get on with It." HBR.org, June 7, 2011. https://hbr.org/2011/06/collaboration-is-risky-now-get.

Are you worried that your coworker is slacking off? Is someone exploiting your ignorance about one topic and stealing your ideas about another? It's hard to build trust in a virtual collaboration when you can't get an in-person read on the other person's character. Johnson offers universal advice for overcoming these fears and embracing an open, generous partnership.

Torres, Nicole. "Just Hearing Your Phone Buzz Hurts Your Productivity." HBR.org, July 10, 2015. https://hbr.org/2015/07/just-hearing-your-phone-buzz-hurts-your-productivity.

When you work remotely, your day is a constant stream of notifications: ringtones, chirps, buzzes, and pop-up boxes. Learn how these alerts damage your focus, slow down your work, and even introduce errors in your performance.

Watkins, Michael. "Remote Leadership: Meeting the Challenge of Working for a Virtual Boss." HBR.org, July 20, 2007. https://hbr.org/2007/07/remote-leadership-meeting-the.

Of all the collaborators you need to stay aligned with, your boss is probably the most important one. But while you can't ignore their e-mails, they might ignore yours. Watkins outlines four key strategies for staying connected with the person who matters most to your work life.

Books

Fried, Jason and David Heinemeier Hansson. *Remote: Office Not Required.* New York: Crown Business, 2013.

Learn from the real-life experiences of the creators of 37signals (now called Basecamp), among other web-based tools, where virtual collaboration is the order of the day. Having built a remote work environment at their own company, Fried and Hansson describe the challenges and benefits of this arrangement. The authors are zealous converts to virtual work and full of relatable stories that show how individual contributors and companies can make this work.

Harvard Business School Publishing. *HBR Guide to Managing Up and Across.* Boston: Harvard Business Review Press, 2013.

The greater the number of remote collaborators your work pulls in, the more likely you are to work with peers and supervisors who don't fit cleanly into an org chart. Even if you're a full-time employee, your virtual coworkers probably come from different departments. This guide helps you learn how to build productive relationships with anyone and advance your agenda—and your career—in the bargain.

Harvard Business School Publishing. *HBR's 10 Must Reads on Emotional Intelligence.* Boston: Harvard Business Review Press, 2015.

As a remote worker, you're operating in a low-information environment when it comes to reading your coworkers' social and emotional cues. To navigate these relationships, you'll need to hone your emotional intelligence (EI)—your ability to perceive and respond to other people's emotional states and your own. Starting with Daniel Goleman's seminal article about EI, "What Makes a Leader?," you'll learn how to evaluate your own EI and regulate the effect of your emotions on your decision making, your professional relationships, and your own well-being.

Articles

Bharadwaj, Sangeeta Shah. "Case Study: Can a Work-at-Home Policy Hurt Morale?" *Harvard Business Review*, April 2015 (product #R1504K).

If you're an occasional, a regular, or a full-time remote employee of a company, this article on the trade-offs of telecommuting will give you a broader picture of what might be happening in your organization. Reflect on how your work arrangements affect your in-office colleagues, and look for ideas you could bring to your own employer to mitigate these problems.

Birkinshaw, Julian and Jordan Cohen. "Make Time for the Work That Matters." *Harvard Business Review*, September 2013 (product #R1309K).

A London Business School professor and a productivity expert share their research-based self-assessment that helps you evaluate all your daily activities. You learn how to decide which ones are not that important to either you or your company and which are relatively easy to drop, delegate, or outsource. Your results will reveal small but significant changes you can make to your day-to-day work schedule to boost your productivity.

Gratton, Lynda and Tamara J. Erickson. "Eight Ways to Build Collaborative Teams." *Harvard Business Review*, November 2007 (product #R0711F).

Teams that work together closely need to overcome the social distance of virtual work more than any other kind of collaborators do, but without constant attention, any bonds formed will deteriorate. In a study of 55 large teams, Gratton and Erickson identified eight success factors, from relationship norms to assignment structures, for collaborative teams. Evaluate your own team's strengths and weaknesses against Gratton and Erickson's model, and brainstorm new practices you can pitch to the group.

Sources

Primary sources for this book

Dillon, Karen. "Managing Remote Relationships." In *HBR Guide to Managing Up and Across* by Harvard Business School Publishing. Boston: Harvard Business Review Press, 2013.

Gallo, Amy. "How to Get Your Colleagues' Attention." HBR.org, May 14, 2015. https://hbr.org/2015/05/how-to-get-your-colleagues-attention.

O'Hara, Carolyn. "5 Ways to Work from Home More Effectively." HBR.org, October 2, 2014. https://hbr.org/2014/10/5-ways-to-work-from-home-more-effectively.

Samuel, Alexandra. "Things to Buy, Download, or Do When Working Remotely." HBR.org, February 4, 2015. https://hbr.org/2015/02/things-to-buy-download-or-do-when-working-remotely.

Other sources consulted

Berry, Paul. "Communication Tips for Global Virtual Teams." HBR.org, October 30, 2014. https://hbr.org/2014/10/communication-tips-for-global-virtual-teams.

Fayard, Anne-Laure and John Weeks. "Who Moved My Cube?" *Harvard Business Review*, July–August 2011 (product #R1107H).

Ferrazzi, Keith. "Get Your Virtual Team Off to a Fast Start." HBR.org, March 18, 2014. https://hbr.org/2014/03/get-your-virtual-team-off-to-a-fast-start.

———. "How to Avoid Virtual Miscommunication." HBR.org, April 12, 2013. https://hbr.org/2013/04/how-to-avoid-virtual-miscommun.

———. "How to Build Trust on Your Virtual Team." HBR.org Video, July 14, 2015. https://hbr.org/video/2363593491001/how-to-build-trust-on-your-virtual-team.

———. "How to Manage Conflict in Virtual Teams." HBR.org, November 19, 2012. https://hbr.org/2012/11/how-to-manage-conflict-in-virt.

———. "How Successful Virtual Teams Collaborate." HBR.org, October 24, 2012. https://hbr.org/2012/10/how-to-collaborate-in-a-virtua.

———. "To Make Virtual Teams Succeed, Pick the Right Players." HBR.org, December 18, 2013. https://hbr.org/2013/12/to-make-virtual-teams-succeed-pick-the-right-players.

———. "Virtual Teams Can Outperform Traditional Teams." HBR.org, March 20, 2012. https://hbr.org/2012/03/how-virtual-teams-can-outperfo.

———. "Working Smoothly with a Virtual Boss." HBR.org, December 11, 2014. https://hbr.org/2014/12/working -smoothly-with-a-virtual-boss.

Harvard Business School Publishing. *HBR Guide to Coaching Employees (eBook + Tools)*. Boston: Harvard Business Review Press, 2014.

———. *HBR Guide to Project Management (ebook + Tools)*. Boston: Harvard Business Review Press, 2015.

———. *Leading Virtual Teams* (Pocket Mentor Series). Boston: Harvard Business School Press, 2010.

Ibarra, Herminia. "Gaining Credibility in a New Role." HBR.org Video, September 24, 2013. https://hbr.org/ video/2227114766001/gaining-credibility-in-a-new-role.

Maruca, Regina Fazio. "How Do You Manage an Off-Site Team?" *Harvard Business Review*, July–August, 1998 (product #3685).

Prusak, Laurence and Don Cohen. "How to Invest in Social Capital." *Harvard Business Review*, June 2001 (product #9381).

Sobel-Lojeski, Karen. "The Subtle Ways Our Screens Are Pushing Us Apart." HBR.org, April 8, 2015. https:// hbr.org/2015/04/the-subtle-ways-our-screens-are -pushing-us-apart.

Spreitzer, Gretchen, Peter Bacevice, and Lyndon Garrett. "Why People Thrive in Coworking Spaces." *Harvard Business Review*, September 2015 (product #F1509A).

Waber, Ben, Jennifer Magnolfi, and Greg Lindsay. "Workspaces That Move People." *Harvard Business Review*, October 2014 (product #R1410E).

Sources

Watkins, Michael. "Making Virtual Teams Work: Ten Basic
Principles." HBR.org, June 27, 2013. https://hbr.org/
2013/06/making-virtual-teams-work-ten.

Watkins, Michael. "Remote Leadership: Meeting the Challenge of Working for a Virtual Boss." HBR.org, July 20,
2007. https://hbr.org/2007/07/remote-leadership
-meeting-the.

Index

Notes

Notes

Notes

Notes

Notes

Notes

Notes

Notes